YOUR KNOWLEDGE HAS VALUE

Bibliographic information published by the German National Library:

The German National Library lists this publication in the National Bibliography; detailed bibliographic data are available on the Internet at http://dnb.dnb.de .

Imprint:

Copyright © 2008 GRIN Verlag, Open Publishing GmbH
Print and binding: Books on Demand GmbH, Norderstedt Germany
ISBN: 9783640508785

This book at GRIN:

http://www.grin.com/en/e-book/139860/teaching-project-lois-lowry-1993-the-giver

Johannes Vees, Michael Bruder, Andreas Jaksch

Teaching Project: Lois Lowry (1993) "The Giver"

GRIN Publishing

GRIN - Your knowledge has value

Since its foundation in 1998, GRIN has specialized in publishing academic texts by students, college teachers and other academics as e-book and printed book. The website www.grin.com is an ideal platform for presenting term papers, final papers, scientific essays, dissertations and specialist books.

Visit us on the internet:

http://www.grin.com/

http://www.facebook.com/grincom

http://www.twitter.com/grin_com

Teaching project designed by:

Michael Bruder, Andreas Jaksch, Johannes Vees

> # *Teaching project*
> # *Lois Lowry: „The Giver"*
> # *(1993)*

Content

1. Synopsis

„The Giver" by Lois Lowry was published in 1993, immediately winning the John Newbery Medal award for excellence in children's literature.

The story takes place in an utopian world. The main character, a twelve-year old boy named Jonas, lives together with his sister Lilly and his parents. However, his parents are not his biological parents as they were chosen by the community to take care of Jonas. Together with his friends Asher and Fiona, Jonas waits for the ceremony of twelve in which every child of that age gets a "job" for his future life. The characters of the novel have no own voice or possibility to design their future - the community predefines their lives.

In the ceremony, Jonas is chosen to be the new "Receiver of Memory".

Jonas doesn't know what lies ahead of him and soon, he meets an old wise man, the so-called "Giver of Memory". The Giver trains Jonas in a certain way: He is the only person in the community who can experience real feelings. By transmitting his knowledge mentally to Jonas, the Giver loses the feelings himself. Jonas does not only experience feelings but also specific things, which aren't present in this world: His first experience is to be sitting on a moving sledge. He likes this memory, not knowing that there are also bad, painful memories to come. His first painful memory is a sunburn. There are also no colours in this novel's world of sameness. Not surprisingly, it's Jonas, who gets the memory of colours from the Giver.

Jonas still lives at home with his parents, of course, he is not allowed to speak about his experiences with them. The family now has a new member, a new child called Gabriel. One day, the Giver offers Jonas to have a look at the so-called release of a new child: Jonas agrees and sees his father with a syringe, killing (or in the novel: releasing) a new child.

Now, Jonas knows the worst secret of the world in which he lives in. When he hears that his little brother Gabriel is about to get released because of insomnia (=sleeplessness), Jonas decides to take over responsibility. He is willing to escape from the community. The Giver explains that a long time ago, everyone had feelings, good and bad ones. He is sure, that, if Jonas can escape from the community, everyone will get back these feelings. Jonas writes a letter to his parents, that he will be back until the next ceremony. He escapes from the world with his little brother to save Gabriel's life. On his way, planes search for him and Gabriel only stops crying when Jonas transmits a nice memory to Gabriel. After a while, Jonas starts to get unsure, whether his decision was correct, but he keeps on escaping until he reaches the top of a hill. Suddenly he hears people singing and he sees lights and colours.

2. General outline

We have decided upon the reading of "The Giver" by Lois Lowry, first published in April of 1993, since we firmly believe in its appropriate applicability in the English Foreign Language Classroom. Due to a lack of experience as teachers, we were not entirely sure about the grade, yet eventually chose to discuss the book in a 9th grade of Realschule. The choice of grade depends both on the language level of the literary source and the content it deals with.

Our very own experiences at school taught us that the language level of books is usually way too high for the class' majority, thus we excluded the type of school called Hauptschule immediately. As there can be found a logical and not too difficult sentence structure throughout the novel, we considered "The Giver" as a suitable challenge for students of Realschule. It's our task as teachers neither to overburden nor to underchallenge students, but to challenge them pertinently. Our groups deems 9th graders of aforesaid type of school capable of dealing with the language used. It goes without saying that there'll be students who may have problems every now and then, but there's no need to grasp the meaning of each and every sentence. Rather is it essential to convey the overall message with the help of regular class discussions and consistent reading tasks.

Concerning the content, the literary category is pretty evident: modern fantasy. All of our group members being enrolled in the subject German as well, we learned about the use of fantasy literature a lot for German lessons. For sure, it can be applied in English as well. Moreover, the preferential age group is independent from the language. According to current pedagogic and didactic literature, fantasy novels seem to be fit for students of 9th grade. There's merely one problematic issue about fantasy literature. Most boys do absolutely love them and are quite logically very eager to read them, no matter which language is applied. However, the reading must be chosen very cautiously due to girls' first aversion towards fantasy literature. Above all do they usually dislike literature that deals with shooting in the universe and outer space topics in general. Here's the ace in the hole of Lowry's fantasy novel. Even though having its setting in a futuristic and superficial utopian society, its main message mediates the need for more emotional depth in communities and societies – criticizing lambency over all. Especially girls are very sensitive about such issues and can thus easily be persuaded by the book. Hence we think there's only a small peril within a 9th grade to have students who entirely refuse to engage in the reading.

On the whole, the plot is enunciated on a comprehensible level and the language is written in such a way that it can be grasped in the majority of cases. Basically, the novel is intended to be read individually most of the time, even though we find it fundamental to offer class reading on scheduled time segments.

With reference to the curriculum that came into force in 2004, there are some aspects to be emphasized:[1]

Students can absorb fictional texts of intermediate level of difficulty by reading; they can make the content accessible and understand the context (p. 80)

Students can reproduce, circumscribe, structure, investigate and work on the text's gist (p. 80)

Students can communicate age-appropriate on the following topics: society; societal change; societal problems; youth and youth culture (p. 80)

Students can work with a bilingual dictionary (p. 81)

Document and present data and facts with traditional and modern media of presentation (p. 81)

3. Literary approach

Literature today is supposed to concentrate on history and characteristics of literary movements, as well as on a text's social, historical or political background. Moreover, information on the author and the period of time it was written are relevant. Such aspects might help to enhance the understanding as a whole. In advance, a teacher is always anxious about whether the learners are interested in the content of the literary source and whether they dispose of the required language skills.

There are currently three major literary approaches under implementation. The cultural approach was at once ruled out by us since we considered it understandably inept for our procedural method. To tell the truth, we had some problems to match our teaching ideas with a corresponding literary approach. For this reason, we decided on a mixture of the personal and language-based approach. Both of them contain precious perceptions, as we would like to demonstrate:

---

[1] Kultus und Unterricht – Bildungsplan für die Realschule, 2004. Lehrplanheft 1/2004. Villingen-Schwenningen: Neckar-Verlag, pp. 80-81.

Personal approach (personal growth)	Language-based approach

Overall teaching objective: engage students personally; thus cause them to read for pleasure and personal fulfillment
 	
Characteristics:
 	
Reading as an individual experience
Student-centered
Development of critical abilites (→personal growth)
Literary text as a resource
Enjoyable reading (appreciate literature)
Generate language skills
 	
    ➢ Criticism:
 	
No real possibility to assess students' learning process
Stylistic are neglected
	Overall teaching objective: improvement of English language
	
	Characteristics:
	
	Involves ability to analyze a text
	Shows stylistics in a text (e.g. hypotaxis)
	Rather teacher-centered
	Dealing with language on an abstract level
	
	    ➢ Criticism:
	
	Sometimes text is too difficult (more translating than working with the source)
	Lack of methodology

4. Routines

We did explicitly not mention the daily routines the students are confronted with while working with the text in our lesson plans.

There'll be enough time spent during every lesson to resolve vocabulary which is essential and hard to look up for students at home. Yet, it is important to have students take over responsibility for vocabulary by either learning all words obstinately and without any carelessness or by looking up unfamiliar terms in a monolingual dictionary – a bilingual one would be even better, but it falls short of the purpose in 9th grade of Realschule. Either way develops methodological competences within each students – one out of four areas of competence in the Bildungsplan 2004 in Baden-Württemberg.

Besides, every chapter must be summarized briefly while or after reading it. Students have to draw such a pattern and complete it continuously during their course of reading (no more than five sentences per box!):

Chapter	Characters	summary	Your opinion
1			
2			
3			

All of us are convinced of this reading method since we got the chance to experience in during our own school career. It's usually not a great deal to fill out the boxes, therefore students don't feel lots of burden by this constant homework. Every now and then, it's annoying, yet most students quickly realize how useful it is for them. Its aim is to enable personal access to novels in particular. It allows students to find an individual working speed with literature. The reader is "invited" to contribute his/her personal feelings and views upon the respective content of a chapter. The longer the text, the more often can the reading diary be consulted to look up contents of previous chapters.

5. Lesson plans

In our first lesson, we want to introduce the book with the topic "A perfect day/ A perfect life". The world of Jonas seems to be perfect. Everything is under control, there is no war or fear or pain and every person is assigned a role in the community. The fact that this world is by far not perfect is to be discovered later when Jonas receives his memories from the Giver.

As the students get a first impression of the book, we want to give them background information on the author of this fictional book. First, we want to discuss what the children might think about the author. Besides, we believe that students always should know a few facts about the author of a novel which is read in class. We also want to have a closer look at the writing style in the novel. This could possibly be a difficult exercise for some students, but we want to give them an idea how they can improve or change their writing style.

Later, we want to have a closer look at the topic "diversity and sameness". The whole world of Jonas is based on sameness. The world doesn't allow diversity, for example every boy gets a new, short haircut, which exposes his ears after the ceremony of tens. Our students should collect ideas to justify their opinion in a discussion. In the end, everyone should build its own opinion on this topic. With this exercise, we also want the pupils to improve their oral language skills.

Our next lesson is all about the characters of the novel- as a teacher, we want to get an impression of the pupils' knowledge about the characters. Further, we want to put our focus on Jonas's character progress during the first chapters. At the end of this lesson, we want to connect the students' knowledge with their everyday life by asking if any of the characters in the novel reminds the students of somebody in their real life.

In the next lesson, our students are to play the roles of members of the community. Students show their knowledge about the characters and practise their oral skills in a funny way. With the help of this amusing game, we also want to encourage the students to keep on reading the novel (at home).

We also want to have a look at the motives in the novel.

For example: The students discover, like Jonas, the true meaning of the word "release" in the book. As we want to work with the *whole* class, everyone gets a part of a word, which, as soon as it is named, is to be written on the board.

Jonas wants to escape from the community.

We want to know the predictions of the students. What could happen now?

Later, we want the them to imagine to be in a similar situation. They explain what they might take with them.

In our last lesson, we want to discuss the ending of the book as it is unclear, whether the ending scene was from Jonas' memory or reality. We also want to take Lois Lowry's description of the novel into consideration. Small groups discuss the description of the book and give a short presentation afterwards.

As a conclusion, we think that it is important that students express their feeling about the novel. This would be our final homework. We would like to collect these opinions in the next lesson, so that we know, whether this book is appropriate for teenagers in 9th grade.

6. Sources

Kultus und Unterricht – Bildungsplan für die Realschule, 2004. Lehrplanheft 1/2004. Villingen-Schwenningen: Neckar-Verlag

Internet sources

➢ http://faculty.salisbury.edu/~elbond/giver.htm (date: 06/11/2008)

➢ http://www.4teachers.de (date: 06/25/2008)

➢ http://www.mce.k12tn.net/reading17/giver.htm (date: 06/11/2008)

➢ http://www.theliterarylink.com/giver_lessons.html (date: 06/25/2008)

YOUR KNOWLEDGE HAS VALUE

- We will publish your bachelor's and master's thesis, essays and papers

- Your own eBook and book - sold worldwide in all relevant shops

- Earn money with each sale

Upload your text at www.GRIN.com
and publish for free